# CONFESSING CHURCH

# Confessing Church

## A Movement is at Hand

**CHRIS LEE**

Liberty Coalition Publications

# CONTENTS

This work is dedicated my wife Liza - who never stops believing in me - and my two children, Demi and EJ.

# Preface

**(Jared Gustafson)**

"Si vis pacem para bellum." I wish I could say that I memorized these words in boot camp, training for some epic war between good and evil. In reality, I heard them watching the movie The Punisher as a teenager, hoping that the time would come where I would be enlisted to fight for a worthy cause. "Si vis pacem para bellum." This is Latin for "if you want peace, prepare for war."

This statement has always resonated with me for some unexplainable reason, but it has never gripped me as strongly as it has this last year. Twenty-twenty has felt a lot like a postapocalyptic scene from a disaster movie. And it is not just because I have been in and out of military-grade war tents on the frontlines of covid-19, or because I have bagged several more bodies than usual in the emergency room where I work. It's felt this way because, in addition to a pandemic, we have witnessed a tumultuous and chaotic social/political landscape. Protests, rioting, and looting swept across the country, and we even witnessed downtown Seattle get sieged by radical left ideologues who announced a new nation called "CHAZ."

These protests spawned conversations surrounding

historical oppression, police brutality, privilege, systemic racism, and even called into question the foundation and values of our nation. While many of these conversations intrigued me, I was aghast at some of the rhetoric. Protestors held signs that read "f*ck white America." Shouts that could be regularly heard included "f*ck the police" and "fry pigs like bacon." To gain greater understanding and insight, I even joined a protest. Pleasantly surprised by some demonstrators but unnerved by others, I left desperately wanting peace but somehow braced for war.

And if the incredibly complex conversation regarding race relations wasn't enough to occupy my time and attention, discussions ensued surrounding covid-19: pending economic collapse, the restrictions to our civil liberties, the social ramifications of shutting down schools, churches, and businesses, and the inevitable consequences if we were not to shut down. Throw in a little banter around the tensest presidential election in US history, a small chat about QAnon, and a snide remark about civil war to top it all off, and you got yourself one heck of a year.

Understandably, this year has left me rattled and shaken. I often have more questions than answers: How do I support my black friends? How do I support my friends in law enforcement? Do I post the black square or do I not? Do I wear a mask and socially distance? Can I attend a church service and a family gathering without being labeled a "super spreading germ factory"? Can I vote for Trump and not be racist? Can someone vote for Biden and not be a socialist? Which "experts" are actually right? Can

I say, "Ellen Page is a good actress" without being labeled a "poisonous bigot"? In a world polarized and unhinged, how do we come together?

Amidst all of these questions, resides a deeper question, still! As a Christian, I ask myself "How does the gospel of Jesus direct me in the year of 2020?" "What does it mean to follow Christ and reveal him to the world?" As I survey Christendom, I see some pastors almost ignoring social/political issues, seemingly hopeful that the problems we face will just go away so they can get back to "church as usual." Are we meant to be proverbial ostriches with our head in the sand, blind to what's happening around us? Has the gospel of Jesus lost all real connection with the material world? This idea leaves me thinking that the gospel is not relevant but is somehow disconnected from my life and human experience.

On the other hand, some pastors have decided to climb aboard popular slogans and social narratives, pushing against the conservative right or "rightwingers." I've seen emboldened young leaders across the country revolt against traditionally evangelical allegiances trying to stay "woke" and relevant. I recently sat through a church service where the entire message was devoted to race relations and better understanding "white privilege." Are these conversations bringing us together and unifying the body of Christ? Or are they more akin to franchises and corporations across the nation cowering to the demands of the progressive popular opinion, not wanting to lose their platform and following?

If these conversations are truly meant to bring us together, why do they perpetually emphasize our differences leaving us feeling more disconnected, separated, and divided? On the basis that I am a white male, I sense that I am cast in a role not of my choosing. As society talks about race and gender, I feel that I am playing the part of the oppressor. One day, I realized I try to prove that I am not racist. As if it's not enough to simply live, love, and be free in the good news of Jesus. I am required to intentionally renounce racism and be "anti-racist" otherwise I am accused of "passively contributing to systemic oppression." I attempt to emerge as a powerful contributor in the world, but on the basis of my race and gender I am regarded with great suspicion as if I am contributing to the same tyrannical power that has oppressed others for centuries.

It is with my many questions and mixed up emotions that I read "Confessing Church" by Chris Lee. This short but powerful book left me hopeful and inspired. It redirected my gaze to the relevant and pertinent gospel of Jesus. Amidst a world emphasizing racial identity and categorical differences, Chris brings the focus back onto our unity in Jesus. The many questions surrounding faith seemed simplified as I was released to enjoy my union with God and humanity.

Chris brilliantly covers areas of church history that correspond with our modern world. Historical heroes are highlighted such as Dietrich Bonhoeffer and his resistance to the Church Reich Administration in Nazi, Germany. The theories and philosophies that undergird much of our progressive narratives are exposed as futile and divisive in contrast with the glad message of Jesus. This book is so incredibly hopeful that one might mistake it for a work of fiction. But it's all too true.

And this piece is written by a man who truly embodies this message. As a best friend of mine for nearly a decade, I have witnessed Chris' unconditional positive regard for humanity that with regularity manifests as unbridled passion! I have witnessed his faithful service to diverse people groups from the bush of Africa to all across the USA. He is a loving father, faithful friend, and integral businessman.

After reading this book, I am more settled about this phrase: "Si vis pacem para bellum." The message contained within this book empowers my peace and awakens my warrior spirit.

# Foreword

**(Randolph Lee JR)**

If you love Me, keep My Commands' (Jn.14:15), stated the Savior to His disciples. To love the Lord is to keep the teachings of His Word...

A wise Bible teacher once told his student, 'if you can be remembered for anything, be remembered for being biblical.' In other words, 'be uncompromising in essential matters of the Christian Faith, and uncompromising in essential matters of moral conduct.' The student then, following closely to the advice of his teacher, began to keep the habit of consistently checking his actions against the Scriptures, as opposed to the culture around him.

In short time, the student found himself on the receiving end of mockery and ridicule by even those who sought his advice. This wasn't so bad, and in fact, the student had been forewarned that it was to be expected. To this end, the student embraced the daily slings-and-arrows as evidences of the fact that he had been set on a right road, and his teacher had not advised amiss.

It was not long, however, before confusion began to set in which bred continual troubles to the student's mind and disrupted the tranquility which had to then been cultivated in his soul. Having set his feet on the path of righteousness that every Christian Soldier must trod, he had fully expected, even anticipated, that he would be declaring himself an adversary of the World.

The World was well-known to be terrible of temperament and unforgiving in nature. She had a hard way about her and demanded total allegiance, although she never really could promise anything in return that was substantial in value. Her realm was purely temporal, and her promised pleasures were most often short-lived and at times offered nothing more rewarding than pain for the trouble of their pursuits. She was a demanding master to those who chose to serve her, and it was for this reason that the student did not entertain many ideas regarding friendly treatment from the World, for if she could be so harsh to those who sacrificed their lives in her service, how much greater would she be expected to set herself against those who refused her offers and advances.

That the World would level mockery at the young student came to him then as no surprise. However, the day had arisen in which the World seemingly found an unlikely ally in the Church, and this was very nearly intolerable. That the same Church which had nourished him up with the sweet mother's milk of the Body and Blood, while washing him clean in baptismal waters of Amazing Grace, would turn Her back to him was an idea too great to tolerate.

With anxiety so magnificent in his mind that his physical flesh began to ache, the student returned to his teacher. For the first time in forever, even the Scriptures themselves seemed to provide no sanctuary for his troubled soul.

'Teacher,' he began, 'I followed your advice, and never did I feel uncertain. I reflected often on the demands of Christ to keep His commands, and thereby ensured that always was I known for being biblical. I strove to speak truth with the grace befitting a saint and to season my speech with the gratitude becoming an adopted son. Above all, I was 'uncompromising in essential matters of Faith and essential matters of conduct,' and for these things was I almost certainly promised, and almost certainly prepared for, conflict with the World. Truly, I strove daily to deny myself the comfort of seeking her approval, though it had been easier at times would I have done so. Now then, tell me what I am to think when, having steadfastly stood strong all this time, I now see the same Church I would have sacrificed my life for, setting Herself against me to stand in solidarity with the Seductress!'

Contrary to showing concern or even sympathizing with his student, the teacher appeared somewhat amused as he spoke, 'Son, you have long allowed the words of the Savior to guide your walk, that if you love me you will keep my commands. And this for good reason! How else were it possible that men should either come to admire you, or come to accuse you, for being biblical? Now then, is it not written in John 14-and-1, let not your heart be troubled? I assure you, the Harlot you confuse as Holy is not the same Bride of Christ our Redeemer that has long nurtured you and I this great many years. While churches may persecute you for sake of the Word, the Church will suffer alongside you and guard your soul in Her bosom.'

'But the Church is currently crumbling beneath the weight of societal demands, and cowering before cultural pressures-,' the student began. 'The devil away from you and repent of such a thought!' the teacher interjected, 'Is it not also written in Matthew 16-and-18 that the gates of Hell shall not prevail against Her?!'

'Let not your heart be troubled,'(Jn.14:1) declared the Messiah to the Church through the declaration to His disciples. The Carpenter understood the foundations of that which they were building would be so solid that 'not even the gates of Hades would prevail against it' (Matt.16:18).

Arguably, all that is representative of true Christianity could be taken and condensed into just a few essential articles of faith and conduct. While there is a very great deal that can be left to individual conscience, and the benefit of personal liberty extended to all in the deciding of amoral matters for themselves, there are unquestionably certain doctrinal and ethical musts that require the agreement and adherence of the individual that declares themselves a member of the body of Christ.

If I consider myself a Christian (which is to say, a follower of Christ), I must accept that Jesus of Nazareth is the Messiah, the Son of the Living God (Matt.16:16).

If I consider myself a Christian (which is to say, a follower of Christ), I must accept that all are created in the image of God, with inherent worth and dignity (Gen.1:26-27).

If I consider myself a Christian (which is to say, a follower of Christ), I must by necessity reject ideologies and teachings which are irreconcilable with (and even damnable by) Scripture which instructs in righteousness (2Tim.3:16).

There is a requirement on behalf of believers (and especially those who consider themselves teachers and leaders) to uncompromisingly stay true to the Word, and never prostitute Scripture by yoking it's doctrinal and ethical mandates with ideas and philosophies which are worthy of no higher position than that which could be afforded through the pits of Tartarus.

As the Preacher once stated, there is no new thing under the Sun (Eccl.1:9). Similarly, old heresies do not simply relegate themselves to the ash heaps of history, only to be glimpsed and examined by the prying eyes of scholars. Old heresies, and especially old and effective heresies, are recycled and often rebranded for the sake of destroying purity to the greatest degree they are able. It doesn't require a great deal of effort to recognize this, if there is honesty in examination and reflection.

If I would refuse to condemn the practices of the modern abortion clinic, and especially the practice of partial-birth infanticide, I must not condemn the practices of Nazi Germany too strongly.

If I would refuse to speak out regarding Critical Race Theory today, I must not condemn too strongly the race theories of Nazi Germany, either.

If I would refuse Christ today, as revealed in Scripture to be the Messiah, I must not criticize any other too harshly for making Him into whatever they needed Him to be...

...throughout the entirety of world history.

There are demands placed upon every individual wishing to embrace the declarations of liberty. A thief cannot be truly free until such a time as he abstains from stealing, cheating, and fraud. An adulteress cannot know the peace of a satisfied conscience while making her marriage bed into a lodge for sojourners. To experience the pleasures of liberty, there are sacrifices that must be made, and continually so. Even a good man, having done his best to walk in the paths of virtue, and forsake the vices which called to him in his youth, will sometimes feel the pains of self-denial in the face of temptation.

The declaration always comes with a demand in this instance. Yet, there are some shepherds who, not unlike those Ezekiel prophesied against (Ez.34:2), continue feeding themselves when they are intended to feed the flocks. There is, perhaps, an even more tempting and dangerous substance to gorge upon than money and material wealth for those who find themselves in positions of leadership, and that is approval.

Seeking approval, when it comes at the expense of remaining ethical, is one of the truest roads to damnation. Cuba was once an island paradise. Now look at it. Having had occasion to once hear an acquaintance tell of the thing, the communist takeover required the removal of a very large obstacle before it could be fully successful. This acquaintance stated, with tears in her eyes and pain in her voice, that 'Castro needed the pastors and priests to tell us all that it was okay. The pastors and priests told us all that it would be for our good, and that was the end of everything. Once that happened, the people became accepting and Cuba fell to communism.'

I never asked details of her story, such as when she fled, or how she came (by the grace of God!), to American shores. I never spoke to her about it, yet I know for a certainty that she wanted the message heard. As she stood in the midst of the small Pentecostal congregation, and made her declaration for freedom, she also offered a very specific demand to any shepherd who would hear her voice. Her message was simply this. 'Never compromise the truth. The very lives of your flock may depend upon your commitment to it!'

I feel compelled in the interests of being biblical to address a regrettable critique that often arises with regards to the subject of socialism or communism, and their alleged scriptural endorsement found in the New Testament. While an individual unfamiliar with the Scriptures ought rightly be commended for raising the question, I find it nearly intolerable coming from those who consider themselves teachers within the Church, as there is no real excuse for the blasphemous mistake.

In truth, there are leaders who do not raise the subject with any honest inquisitiveness, but rather as a lead-in to radical propositions which prove either their lunacy or naivety. The Acts of the Apostles do not in any way promote communism as an acceptable governmental or political model in the 2nd and 4th chapters. Yes, it is true that all things were had in common by the earliest believers following Pentecost (Acts4:32). However (and this is a very big however), the giving, sharing, and distributing of property was a completely volitional act arising from a consensual agreement entered into by each individual. There was no forced confiscation of wealth or tyrannical suppression of members subjugated under threat of the sword.

When immersing the mind in the text itself, and the soul in the consistent imagery of joy and pleasure found briefly in the closing of the 2nd and 4th chapters of Acts, it becomes impossible to confuse these events with the pain and sorrow wrought by those secular governmental and economical systems of which it has been said, 'you can vote your way into, but you will have to shoot your way out.'

Truly, a wise man learns from his mistakes. An even wiser man learns from the mistakes of others. Life is too short to figure and sort everything by personal trial-and-error. History and Tradition are sure guides in the pursuit and cultivation of liberty in all respects. We would be wise to open our hearts, and receive as nourishment to our souls, the wisdom that has passed down and endured through the ages.

May freedom forever ring…

'Men can never be secure from tyranny, if there be no means to escape it till they are perfectly under it: and therefore it is, that they have not only a right to get out of it, but to prevent it.' -John Locke 2$^{nd}$ Treatise of Government

# Introduction

The Gospel of Jesus Christ is the most relevant message in the modern world. It is the Gospel after all, which gives our created order relevance. The material of the Gospel is not merely information, it is the person of the Eternal Son of God, wrapped in humanity's flesh. "It is Him we proclaim."

Jesus, when speaking to His disciples, says, "The words I speak to you are Spirit. They are life." The need for the gospel is not simply a need for information about God; it is a need for Spirit and Life. It is the need for one's soul to be shaken from its slumber, to look around and see as did Jacob, "The Lord was here and I knew it not!" The need for the hearing of the Gospel is that of a child to know the face of the love which raised him or her up - while yet without comprehension or strength to walk.

While certain messages disguise themselves in a cloak of justice and goodwill, if a message leans not, on the foundation of Christ and his accomplishments on our behalf such a message is meaningless. We need the sustenance of the bread of life which comes down from heaven to give life to the world. We need the fresh words proceeding from His mouth in the light of His logic which reveals us in Christ, established in the love of the Father.

We need Christ and Him Crucified. Only through the torn veil of His Flesh do we see life and find satisfaction. At different times throughout history, an evangelical desire has led the Church into the pit-fall of a quest for relevance. This has often led to the abandonment of the goodness of the glad message of Jesus Christ. We will explore how this struggle has manifested itself throughout history and stand under the weight of our current cultural struggles together. Through it all we will see that we have everything we need for life and godliness in Christ.

# | 1 |

# Nazi Coordination

"First they came for the communists, and I did not speak out - because I was not a communist.
Then they came for the trade unionists, and I did not speak out - because I was not a trade unionist.
Then they came for the Jews, and I did not speak out - because I was not a Jew.
Then they came for me - and there was no one left to speak for me."

(Martin Neimoller)

## The Evangelical Nazi

The German Government had landed firmly in control of the National Socialist Workers Party, also known as the Nazi party. In order to effect culture to the degree which the party desired, they fixed their sights upon the Evangelical Church. The year was 1930 when the Government rolled out its Gleichschaltung, meaning bring into line or coordination.

Gleichschaltung was a doctrine which was meant to bring the church into line with Nazi ideals. The Old Testament was devalued, Biblical Jesus rejected, and Christocentric teaching was replaced with race-based education. In many churches, the cross was taken down. It was offensive to Bring-Into-Line ideologies.

God was not weak. Men were not meek. Jesus may have been crucified, but the Spirit in which He bore our sins was disgraceful. According to the Gleichschaltung, men were strong — made for war. Adolph Hitler believed that Christian teachings produced "flabby men". To be fair to that thought, there are a lot of flabby men in the Church. There is not a lot we can do about that.

When the Bring-Into-Line doctrine was introduced, you could imagine the opposition it faced. You would have to imagine, because that opposition didn't occur until 1934. For four years the doctrine ran rampant in the Church all throughout Germany.

Did the Government force the Church to embrace the

doctrine? By no means. The coordination was welcomed as a path forward. How exciting it must have been! The Church had the opportunity to coordinate with the young governing regime in shaping its nation's future! However, not all coordination is good coordination, as not all shaping is good shaping. Many weak pastors, lost in a storm of culture, grabbed hold of that golden chalice and drank the magic potion with delight.

Thus the German Evangelical Churches were rapidly transformed into Nazi Education Centers.

## A History of Church Struggle

Throughout Church History, where heresy is established, the Spirit of Truth is responsible, in divine love, to stir up a struggle pursuant to the Truth. Conquerors are revealed. If needs be, they will not be found to love their own lives so much as to cower from death.

Ignatius and Polycarp, both students of the Apostle John, defended the faith from heresy in the 1st century church. Ignatius's fight was the Gnostic worldview which rendered the physical realm irredeemable and thus denied the humanity of Jesus. We think about such messages as biblical heresies, but this message was in the culture of Jesus's time.

The world that Jesus was born into was the known Roman World. Rome was full of mythology regarding gods who visited earth, created storms, and brought wrath. They had stories of gods who laid with human beings and created half-god, half-man demigods. By no means however, could God enter the material world, and become that material. In the Roman mind, that would make Him defiled and not a god at all.

This heresy Ignatius hit head on. He destroyed this ideology in plain sight and landed himself firmly in chains. He celebrated his chains and prayed for the opportunity to give full witness to Jesus in martyrdom. The Church at Rome had political sway and advocated for Ignatius's release. Ignatius wrote to the church, however, and with many words convinced them to get out of the way of his pursuit of a "perfect love". Ignatius detailed in one such letter to the church that he had actually hoped that his torture be so gruesome that nothing would remain of his physical body. His hopes were that those who accompanied him to Rome would not have to carry his body across land and sea to bury him. He received his wish when sentenced to face the wild beast in the arena. Nothing was left of Ignatius but what could be carried in a small jar.

Polycarp, also a student of the Apostle John, was known as the Destroyer of Pagans. At the age of 90, he was burned at the stake in the public square. When the people viewed the public execution of such a feeble and aged frame, they were horrified. Governing powers were shaken by the public response and the church experienced a time of peace.

Martin Luther uncovered a thousand-year-old trap when he questioned the established doctrine that Salvation does not exist outside of the Holy Roman Catholic Church. Martin Luther ascended to glory as an old man in his bed; however, a number of his sojourners were burned at the stake. We see many times throughout church history that the struggle was real.

Let's now return to 1934 and the German Church Struggle of Nazi, Germany.

## German Church Struggle

Four years the Bring-Into-Line coordination ran wild in the German Evangelical Church, tormenting the souls of those Orthodox Christian Protestants who loved participating in the orthodoxy of Christian faith. In the Spring of 1934, the Church Reich Administration had been so emboldened with their success that they may have motioned one motion too far. A ban was decreed throughout the German Evangelical Church which forbade pastors from marrying interracially and equally disqualified pastors from the ministry who had married interracially. At this, one young pastor by the name of Dietrich Bonhoeffer had seen enough.

Bonhoeffer was a student of the famed 20th-century theologian Karl Barth. He leveraged that relationship. After many letters in correspondence with Barth, Bonhoeffer organized a coalition of pastors. He named the coalition the Pastor's Emergency League.

In May of 1934, the Pastor's Emergency League convened for a three-day conference in Barman, Germany, together with Barth, to coordinate a solid resistance to the heresies of the Church Reich. One Biblical scholar wrote of the conference, "It was nothing less than revolution." After three days of deliberating, the Pastor's Emergency League emerged with a document they called the Barman Declaration. The declaration condemned the violence the Church Reich Administration was bringing upon the unity of the German Evangelical Church and confronted the heresies of the coordination with the weight of salvation. Barth, who penned the declaration, said the work "had been fortified by bold coffee and fine Brazilian cigars."

From the declaration flowed a new Christian Movement with fresh blood and a burning revelation. A church was born, which was rightly named the Confessing Church. The church gained its name from its emphasis placed upon the confessing of Jesus Christ. The church cherished a shared unity with all who confessed Christ, with a supreme focus upon Christ alone. This stood in direct opposition to the Church Reich Administration's anti-Christ, race-based propaganda.

A line was drawn in the sand. On one side of the line stood those who held Christ as supreme. They historically became known as the Orthodox German Protestants. On the other side of the line stood those who held race as supreme. They historically became known as the German Christians. Thus a firm resistance had been established with the stature of Christ in the face of the blood thirsty beast.

Eleven years the Church Struggle continued until the collapse of the entire National Socialist party and movement. As a reward for his great service, in April of 1943, Bonhoeffer was arrested by the Gestapo and two years later on April 9th, 1945, Dietrich Bonhoeffer was hanged at the Flossenburg Concentration Camp. He was hanged just days before

United States forces liberated the camp. His final words are recorded, "This is the end, for me the beginning of life."

It truly was the end, as two weeks later the Nazi resistance officially surrendered at Berlin. The party had folded and, with it, the Church Reich Administration. The Bring-Into-Line coordination became seen for what it was. Pastors as well as congregants throughout the nation openly denounced the heresies of the doctrine and there was reconciliation in the Church.

## A Line in the Sand

A line remains in the sand, drawn throughout history. Jesus said, "All who stand on the side of Truth listen to My voice." As we have seen thus far, siding with the truth does not allow us to be indecisive or weak. Sometimes, for the sake of love, it demands that we stand opposite those we care most about.

Christian love is not classically defined as pandering sensitivity, rather "Love" has a name. In Christ, Love became incarnate and lives forevermore in human form. (Selah!) Being so, the most unloving thing we can do for our immediate sphere of influence is allow the unchallenged drift into endless obscurity. In standing your ground, many will call your love hate and your sensitivity to His Voice insensitive.

We will find in our day and age the echoing of the voice of the martyrs, "Defend the faith." Should we respond? "Come" Jesus says, "Hear My voice. Know Me, that you may live."

## Barman Declaration

"In view of the errors of the "German Christians" and of the present Reich Church Administration, which are ravaging the Church and at the same time also shattering the unity of the German Evangelical Church, we confess the following evangelical truths:

1. "I am the Way and the Truth and the Life; no one comes to the Father except through me." John 14:6 "Very truly, I tell you, anyone who does not enter the sheepfold through the gate but climbs in by another way is a thief and a bandit. I am the gate. Whoever enters by me will be saved." John 10:1,9 Jesus Christ, as he is attested to us in Holy Scripture, is the one Word of God whom we have to hear, and whom we have to trust and obey in life and in death. We reject the false doctrine that the Church could and should recognize as a source of its proclamation, beyond and besides this one Word of God, yet other events, powers, historic figures and truths as God's revelation.

2. "Jesus Christ has been made wisdom and righteousness and sanctification and redemption for us by God." 1 Cor. 1:30 As Jesus Christ is God's comforting pronouncement of the forgiveness of all our sins, so, with equal seriousness, he is also God's vigorous announcement of

his claim upon our whole life. Through him there comes to us joyful liberation from the godless ties of this world for free, grateful service to his creatures. We reject the false doctrine that there could be areas of our life in which we would not belong to Jesus Christ but to other lords, areas in which we would not need justification and sanctification through him.

3. "Let us, however, speak the truth in love, and in every respect grow into him who is the head, into Christ, from whom the whole body is joined together." Eph. 4:15-16

The Christian Church is the community of brethren in which, in Word and Sacrament, through the Holy Spirit, Jesus Christ acts in the present as Lord. With both its faith and its obedience, with both its message and its order, it has to testify in the midst of the sinful world, as the Church of pardoned sinners, that it belongs to him alone and lives and may live by his comfort and under his direction alone, in expectation of his appearing.

We reject the false doctrine that the Church could have permission to hand over the form of its message and of its order to whatever it itself might wish or to the vicissitudes of the prevailing ideological and political convictions of the day.

4. "You know that the rulers of the Gentiles lord it over them, and their great ones are tyrants over them. It will not be so among you; but whoever wishes to have authority over you must be your servant." Matt. 20:25-26

The various offices in the Church do not provide a basis for some to exercise authority over others but for the ministry [lit., "service"] with which the whole community has been entrusted and charged to be carried out.

We reject the false doctrine that, apart from this ministry, the Church could, and could have permission to, give itself or allow itself to be given special leaders [Führer] vested with ruling authority.

5. "Fear God. Honor the Emperor." 1 Pet. 2:17

Scripture tells us that by divine appointment the State, in this still unredeemed world in which also the Church is situated, has the task of maintaining justice and peace, so far as human discernment and human ability make this possible, by means of the threat and use of force. The Church acknowledges with gratitude and reverence toward God the benefit of this, his appointment. It draws attention to God's Dominion [Reich], God's commandment and justice, and with these the responsibility of those who rule and those who are ruled. It trusts and obeys the power of the Word, by which God upholds all things.

We reject the false doctrine that beyond its special commission the State should and could become the sole and total order of human life and so fulfill the vocation of the Church as well.

We reject the false doctrine that beyond its special commission the Church should and could take on the nature, tasks and dignity which belong to the State and thus become itself an organ of the State.

6. "See, I am with you always, to the end of the age." Matt. 28:20 "God's Word is not fettered." 2 Tim. 2:9

The Church's commission, which is the foundation of its freedom, consists in this: in Christ's stead, and so in the service of his own Word and work, to deliver all people, through preaching and sacrament, the message of the free grace of God.

We reject the false doctrine that with human vainglory the Church could place the Word and work of the Lord in the service of self-chosen desires, purposes and plans.

The Confessing Synod of the German Evangelical Church declares that it sees in the acknowledgment of these truths and in the rejection of these errors the indispensable theological basis of the German Evangelical Church as a confederation of Confessing Churches. It calls upon all who can stand in solidarity with its Declaration to be mindful of these theological findings in all their decisions concerning Church and State. It appeals to all concerned to return to unity in faith, hope and love.

Verbum Dei manet in aeternum.

**The Word of God will last for ever."**

# | 2 |

# The Sum of All Things

"And here at the manifestation of the Son, magic began to be destroyed and all bonds were loosed; and the Ancient Kingdom and the error of evil was destroyed. Henceforward all things were moved together, and the destruction of death was devised and there was commencement of that which was perfected in God." (Saint Ignatius of Antioch A.D. 100)

## 1st Century Jews

"Christ was crucified with both hands outstretched, with one to draw the Ancient people, with the other to draw the Nations." (Saint Athanasius A.D.300)

The 1st century Jewish mind, before Christ, thought a certain way. In the mind of the religious Jew, there were two kinds of people. There were the covenant people of God and the non-covenant people of the nations. The people of the nations, referred to as "gentiles", even included those people from the northern tribes of Israel. The view was developed as such because through the prophet Jeremiah the Lord spoke of Israel and said, "I gave faithless Israel her certificate of divorce and sent her away because of her adulteries." Thus the northern tribes of Israel became, to Judah, a non-covenant people, no better than the nations. This may help us better grasp the elitist view of the pharisee, who says to himself, "Above all people the Lord has chosen me and above all my brothers the Lord has favored me."

This is why the Apostle Paul included his lineage to Benjamin in his declaration of his excellence as a pharisee of pharisees. Benjamin was of the southern territory of Judah and the dwelling place of Jerusalem. Mary, Jesus' mother, was from the lineage of Judah, and, according to the prophecy, by happen-stance gave birth to Jesus in Bethlehem, the City of David. Thus Jesus assumes the name in the book of revelation "The Lion of the tribe of Judah." Jesus, though, was raised in Nazareth; He grew up in the northern Kingdom of Israel. This caused confusion among the religious experts.

The legitimacy of Christ's origins is brought into question all throughout His earthly ministry. "We do not know where this man is from!" Why does this even matter? "Where is your father?" they asked. "We are not born of fornication" the pharisee said, insinuating that Christ was, and not only that His mother engaged in fornication, but that He belonged to the shame of the Northern Kingdom of whom the Lord spoke in Hosea, "Rebuke your mother for she is not my wife and I am not her husband." They were saying, "Your mother is the fornicator; you have no standing with God." And again "Do we not say rightly that you are a Samaritan and have a demon?" Samaria was of the northern territory of Israel.

We know beyond what tribe Christ derived His origins; His origins should have confounded the minds of the learned, because His origins are with both Divinity and humanity. His Father is the Father Almighty and His mother, human Mary. Son of God and Man born of woman in one. The point here is to emphasize the thinking of the Jewish mind in the day and age which Jesus was born. There were two kinds of people, covenant and non-covenant people.

With this in mind, we can better understand Jesus's convincing of Peter in Acts chapter 10, "Why do you call unclean what I have made clean?" and how upset Peter's believing brothers were with him for entering the home of an unclean gentile. Jesus had real barriers to destroy — much larger barriers than those socio-political barriers of the 21st century. The 1st century Jewish mind (before Christ) did not simply believe that every other people were unclean and unfit to associate with; they had every inclination that God endorsed this as truth.

It is important to note there was a real wall of hostility which existed between the two worlds prior to Christ's crucifixion. In Matthew 10 Jesus sends out the 12 and commands them, "Do not enter the cities of the Samaritans." Upon His resurrection, He affirms that the disciples will testify of His name in Judea, Samaria, and the far reaches of the known world. (Acts 1:8) What had happened? What had changed? Truthfully, everything had changed.

As written by Saint Athanasius (A.D.300) "Christ was crucified with both hands outstretched, with one to draw the Ancient people, with the other to draw the Nations." Christ spoke in the presence of Jews and Greeks alike in John 12, saying "When I am lifted up (on the Cross) I will draw all peoples (Nations) to myself." We see that in the body of Christ's flesh something has happened that has encompassed all nations.

After having briefly peered into this paradigm, let us read a writing from the Apostle Paul and allow the apostle's writing to speak for itself:

"You were without Christ, you were utter strangers to God's chosen community, the Jews, and you had no knowledge of, or right to, the promised agreements. You had nothing to look forward to and no God to whom you could turn. But now, through the blood of Christ, you who were once outside the pale are with us inside the circle of God's love and purpose.

For Christ is our living peace. He has made a unity of the

conflicting elements of Jew and Gentile by breaking down the barrier which lay between us. By His sacrifice He removed the hostility of the Law, with all its commandments and rules, and made in Himself out of the two, Jew and Gentile, one new man, thus producing peace. For He reconciled both to God by the sacrifice of one body on the cross, and by this act made utterly irrelevant the antagonism between them. Then He came and told both you who were far from God and us who were near that the war was over." (Ephesians 2:12-18 J.B. Phillips)

## The Pauline Revelation

We can see that something took place in Jesus, a breaking down of indifference. Where there were two, being the Ancient people and the Nations, He brought them into one in Himself - having crucified their enmity.

The apostle Paul writes, "In Christ's family there can be no division into Jew and non-Jew, slave and free, male and female. Among us you are all equal. That is, we are all in a common relationship with Jesus Christ." (Galatians 3:28 MSG) We can see that, where indifference may have once existed, Jesus becomes the common ground. In the apostle Paul's day and age, what could have been more different than the Jew and the non-Jew? Maybe the slave would differentiate more from the free man? Even more, a woman might differentiate from a man, but the apostle expresses an equality that exists in Christ.

The apostle writes again, "Words like Jewish or non-Jewish, religious and irreligious, insider and outsider, uncivilized and uncouth, slave and free, mean nothing. From now on everyone is defined by Christ, everyone is included in Christ." (Colossians 3:11MSG) Something took place in Christ, a re-defining of mankind; a recreating.

Since we are already in over our heads, let us tread just a bit further into the staggering implications of the Pauline revelation. Why the Pauline revelation? It is the Gospel administration which Christ entrusted to the apostle for the Nations and it brings to light how the Father has included the Nations into the fold of His family, His covenant people.

"The love of Christ overmasters us, the conclusion at which we have arrived being this: that One having died for all, His death was their death, and that He died for all in order that the living may no longer live to themselves, but to Him who died for them and rose again. Therefore for the future we know no one simply as a man. Even if we have known Christ as a man, yet we do so no longer. So that if anyone is in Christ, he is a new creature: the old state of things has passed away; a new state of things has come into existence. And all this comes from God, who has reconciled us to Himself through Christ, and has appointed us to serve in the ministry of reconciliation."

After mentioning the ministry of reconciliation, I am sure we will get to hear about His cultural sensitivity services! No, he continues, "WE ARE TO TELL HOW GOD WAS IN CHRIST RECONCILING THE WORLD TO HIMSELF, not charging men's transgressions to their account, and that He has entrusted to us the message of reconciliation." (2 Corinthians 5:14-20) We actually possess the Divinely-derived message which reconciles! Is it possible that we see reconciliation when the Pauline Gospel that includes all people is preached?

The apostle began in this passage saying that One died for all, therefore all died. The One who died and lives again did so that all who live can now be free to march to the beat of a different drum. We are all free to live to Jesus. Free from the dictates of the fallen identity passed down from Adam's error. He goes farther.

No longer do we see any man from a merely human vantage point, as the Lord also counseled Peter who spoke to his brothers, "The Lord has shown me that I must call no man common or unclean." The apostle says we now see from a higher vantage point. And looking, we see that if any one be united with Christ, he or she is a new creature altogether; the old order has passed away and everything is re-ordered. All of this he expresses has come from God, who has reconciled us to Himself in Christ.

The Christian message breaks down barriers. People who would not in a million years enter the same room together are brought to lay down their arms and dine together at the table of the Lord. His voice "breaks the mighty oak." And Christ is the message.

## Why Does This Matter?

When Jesus took off His outer garments, knelt and began washing the feet of His disciples, He declared them to be His guests of honor. Jesus turned our notion of divinity on its head. Jesus then said to His disciples, having washed their feet, "You call Me Teacher and Lord; and you are right for so I am. If I then, the Lord and the Teacher, have washed your feet, you also ought to wash one another's feet." Here, Jesus honored His disciples and liberated them to the joy of honoring one another in the same manner.

Our lives in Christ become enveloped in His divine love. We get to love those around us with the same love with which Christ has loved us. When our hearts have been truly nourished under the wing of Christ's love, we will not consciously love or honor because He has commanded us; His love is simply in us and we are powerless to not love.

Why did He need to demonstrate to Peter so powerfully that he "must call no man common or unclean"? Why did the Spirit reveal to Paul, so completely, all people included in God's redemptive work in Christ? For Paul, the Lord was giving an administration, a message for all people of their inclusion in God's family. For Peter, God was opening his eyes, changing his heart to see as Christ had spoken, "I have other sheep also, and I must bring them and they will listen to My voice. There is one flock and one Shepherd."

The Gospel of Jesus Christ does not demand from us something we do not have; it provides for us more than we've ever needed. The reason this message matters so much to me is because it liberates me to love as I am loved. I have been counseled, as Peter, to call no man "common or unclean." Every person is one whom Jesus bled for.

While each of us is created uniquely by the Father, not one of us is more important than another. The Gospel has liberated my heart to know and understand this. In my day-to-day life as a mixed martial arts coach, as a real estate investor, as a husband and father, this affects my life.

When I am working with someone who is brand new to martial arts, I don't shame him or her because I remember what it was like to be new. He or she is valuable, not simply because of having paid money to be at my training facility, but because I have seen "no man is common". I am not at liberty to treat people like dirt and go to bed at night a happy camper. My conscience is awake to love.

Why does this matter? The Father's desire for our lives is the Fellowship of Jesus — each and every one of us. The Father wants us bursting at the seams in the fellowship or friendship He shares with His Son. He does not want us cooped up in tribal divisiveness or grudges, which weaken our bones and make us sick. The love of the Father cannot truly thrive within a heart in which hatred for our fellow man is still partying.

The Father wants to nourish our bones with the lavish love He pours out upon His Son. He is the God and Father of our Master, Jesus Christ, and Jesus has come to share His God and Father with us. We see this when, after having left the tomb, He encounters Mary Magdalene and tells her, "Go to my brothers and tell them that I go to My God and your God, My Father and your Father." Jesus declared His God to be ours! He declared His Father to be our own!

Jesus has an unbroken fellowship with His God and Father, which He has come to share with us! There is so much more here to explore which we will not do in this work, but this is the heartbeat of the gospel.

Why does this matter? This all matters because the truth

matters. And knowing the truth, we are free to come in and go out in liberty.

# | 3 |

# Ten Steps Backward

"But I resist the devil, and often it is with a fart that I
chase him away."

(Martin Luther)

## A Modern Potion

In the opening of this book we examined the history of what took place in Nazi Germany and the German Evangelical Church's role. We witnessed the replacement of the centrality of Christ with race-based studies. In such a way, we saw many churches effectively become Nazi re-education centers under the guidance of the Church Reich Administration. We witnessed the struggle which followed, continuing until the collapse of the National Socialist Party. We then took a walk about in the glorious inclusive report, the Glad Message of Jesus Christ.

We will now move forward (or backward) into 21st Century Cultural studies, where we will find the grounds laid for the American Church's 21st Century Church Struggle. The main theory we will be discussing in this section is the Critical Race Theory.

Critical race theory (CRT) is "the view that the law and legal institutions are inherently racist and that race itself, instead of being biologically grounded and natural, is a socially constructed concept that is used by white people to further their economic and political interests at the expense of people of color. According to critical race theory (CRT), racial inequality emerges from the social, economic, and legal differences that white people create between "races" to maintain elite white interests in labour markets and politics, giving rise to poverty and criminality in many minority communities."

(Tommy Curry Associate Professor of Philosophy at Texas A&M University.)

At first glance, Critical Race Theory appears to share a remarkable semblance to another famous theory known as Conflict Theory. Conflict Theory starred center stage in the Russian Revolution. The Conflict Theory is the view that society is constantly in a state of conflict. In a given state there is only so much resource to go around, and so a struggle ensues for control of that resource. Those in power seek to maintain control by all means, including the suppressing of the other people.

This theory was developed by Karl Marx. We can see in Conflict Theory people are divided into two sets of people — an oppressor group and an oppressed group. This panned out in Russia in such a way that those people who made less money were turned against those who held more of the resource, namely the farmers who were deemed to be suppressing those less fortunate "Have Nots." Inevitably, the farmers' lands were seized, and many of the farmers were killed.

Looking at Critical Race Theory, it would seem as though it has mirrored Conflict Theory and simply pasted its own definitions as to who the oppressor is and who the oppressed is. This is precisely what has happened. Conflict Theory poses that society is always in conflict between two sets of people — an oppressor people and an oppressed people. Critical Race Theory says the oppressor is White People and the oppressed is People of Color.

## Racial Identity

Critical Race Theory holds that all of life is one big racial power struggle. Every exchange is an exchange in the direction of one race claiming or maintaining racial superiority over another race. According to Critical Race Theory, you are not necessarily consciously doing this; you do it whether you know it or not.

This makes sense of the 2020 push for white people across the United States to proclaim themselves helplessly racist. According to American socialist justice warriors of the year 2020, if you are white, you can be one of two things. You are a racist who acknowledges it, or you are a blind racist who simply cannot see how racist you are. Why white people? Are people of color racist also? According to Critical Race Theorists, the oppressed historically cannot oppress the oppressor, therefore people of color cannot be racist. This is illogical.

If you are white, according to Critical Race Theory, you are an oppressor whether you know it or not. You being you is oppressive to the world around you. Can you imagine this being taught to your children at the elementary school level? That is precisely what has been happening.

Critical Race Theory took center stage in the United States in the year 2020, when President Donald Trump made an executive order to ban the teaching of Critical Race Theory in taxpayer-funded public schools. This was a massive move. He described such an indoctrination of elementary school children as "criminal." There was a massive uproar from leftists all over the country who love to fight for the rights of our children. (Oh, that a boy can be someday a lady, and a girl can be someday a man.)

Again, according to Critical Race Theory, there are two types of people: oppressor and oppressed, white people and people of color. A recent emerging thought from the pail of Critical Race is the deeming as "racist" white people who adopt children of color. How is it racist for white people to adopt children of color? You must see, those white people are imposing their whiteness upon the child of color, erasing from that child of color everything colored about him or her, except the color of his or her skin.

According to Critical Race Theory, because our identity is so tied up with our race, our inner capacity to reason is also tied to our race. Certain thoughts are deemed to be white thoughts, and others are deemed to be thoughts of color. Are thoughts not simply good or bad? Are thoughts really black or white?

In July of 2020 the Smithsonian Institute posted a graphic in its National Museum of African American History and Culture. The graphic read at the top, "Aspects and assumptions of whiteness and white culture." Under the heading it read, "White dominant culture, or whiteness, refers to the ways white people and their traditions, attitudes and ways of life have been normalized over time and are now considered standard practices in the United States. And since white people still hold most of the institutional power in America, we have all internalized some aspects of white culture - including people of color."

Understanding Critical Race Theory helps us understand

what is written here, "white people still hold most of the institutional power in America...". Critical Race Theory continually sets these two groups at odds with each other. In this view white people hold most of the institutional power at the expense of people of color - creating systems that help them maintain elite white supremacy. Does the possibility exist at some point that white people and people of color may live hand-in-hand as Dr Martin Luther King Jr dreamed? Not according to Critical Race Theory. In the world I live in however, people of color and white people share in the table of brotherhood every day.

The graphic goes on to list a number of Aspects and assumptions of whiteness. One aspect the graphic claims to be a very white idea is the notion of the nuclear family. To think that children should grow up in a home with a mother and father present, is an assumption of whiteness. "Objective, rational linear thinking" and "cause and effect relationships" are also constructs of whiteness which are being imposed upon People of Color. Among other things listed are delayed gratification, planning for your future, and respecting authority.

Critical Race Theory sets the stage of society in a state of constant conflict. The white people and people of color are always at enmity, battling for institutional power and resource. Whoever has that power and resource inevitably leverages it over the other.

## No Justice No Peace

Critical Race messaging is very weak in that it has no real

substance. Any movement built upon this foundation will inevitably collapse; the only question is how many casualties it will leave in its wake. As pastors throughout the nation fill the heads of their congregants with such books as White Fragility, How to be an Anti-Racist, and Raising White Kids, I would strongly encourage them to think about the theories which undergird these messages.

Is such a theory conducive to the edification of the body of Jesus Christ? What will the consequences of such a message be? We will look more in depth at this in the upcoming chapter as we contrast the messaging of Critical Race Theory to the Gospel of Jesus Christ. Let us hold everything to the Light.

In May of 2020, if you were a living human in the United States of America, you became familiar with a phrase. Hundreds, in some places thousands, of people filled the streets, protesting "systemic issues", raising their voices for "racial justice". Some protested the United States of America all together. Certain ideas emerged such as the defunding and abolition of the police. A certain chant protestors embraced across the country was "No Justice, No Peace."

Many of the protests turned violent. Forbes reported "14 days of protests, 19 Dead." Some of the protests carried on for as long as five months. The mainstream media reported the protests to be "mostly peaceful" while cities across the U.S. burned. "No justice, no peace."

While violence turned up across the nation, I found myself in shock at the amount of support the riots received from different pastors who pitched in their voices, "Riots are the language of the unheard". In contrast, a coalition of black pastors stood on the courthouse lawn in my home city of Fort Wayne, Indiana, encouraging the public amidst their pain, "Come to the table of reconciliation."

"No justice, no peace" masses raged across the nation. Critical Race Theory poses no peace ever. It presents peace at no time. Always there is conflict, always we are at enmity. One people's success means another people's peril. Never justice, never peace.

# | 4 |

# Glad vs Glum

"See to it that no one takes you captive through philosophy and empty deception, according to the traditions of men, according to the elementary principles of the world, rather than according to Christ. For in Him all the fullness of Deity dwells in bodily form, and in Him you have been made complete."

(Colossians 2:8-10 NAS)

## Glad vs Glum

What more can we add to what the Father has done in His Son? Who will search out the council of the Father, Son, and Spirit that he may instruct them? Is there another way, everlasting? Is there one more fitting than the Son, under whom all things should come together?

In this chapter we will compare and contrast the Glad Message of Jesus Christ to the glum messaging of Critical Race Theory. We will see what common ground does not exist between the two messages. We will examine the glorious empowering message of the Gospel of Christ and find together, we have everything we need.

It is written in Titus 2:11 that, "The grace of God has displayed itself with healing power to all mankind." We are advocating a healing that is for all people everywhere. We have looked at the manner in which Christ tore down the dividing wall of hostility between the Jewish world and the Nations. We have seen how He has established equality of value in Himself irregardless of race, status, or sex. The apostle said, "In Christ's family there can be no division into Jew and non-Jew, slave and free, male and female. Among us you are all equal." (Galatians 3:28MSG)

The gospel brings people together of all different kinds, glorifying them with the dignity which Christ has bestowed upon them. Race, income, status, and sex all take the back seat to Jesus, in whom we derive our identity. Are you a person of color? Great! That is the most perfect color of Christ. Are you a white person? Well that is awesome! Your whiteness is the most perfect color of Christ. You are a uniquely valuable expression of who He is regardless of either.

In Christ we see one new man. Christ makes the case that there is in fact only one race: the human race. This message drastically differs from the nature of a message which divides people up according to the color of their skin. While the gospel unites people of all kinds, Critical Race Theory divides people up according to their kind.

The glad message declares all who identify with Christ to be "more than conquerors". Critical Race Theory holds that white people are more than conquerors of people of color. The glad message declared to those bound in real bonds of slavery, "You are God's free man!" Critical Race Theory declares to a free people of color, "You are oppressed."

The two messages could not be more at odds than Cinderella and her ugly step-sisters.

## We've Got the Power

"This is eternal life," Jesus said, "to know the one true God and Jesus Christ whom He has sent." This knowing Jesus speaks of is an intimate knowing. The word "know" which Jesus chooses to use here is the word ginosko, which means personal, intimate or experiential knowledge.

"His Divine power," the apostle Peter says, "has given us all things toward life and Godliness through the knowledge of the One having called us by His own glory and excellence."

(2 Peter 1:3) The knowledge of God powers our lives. If we possess a personal, experiential, and intimate knowledge of Him who fills all things in every way, what can we be lacking? What can we possibly lack if we have Him and we know it? If we have the knowledge of Christ, what can any worldly system provide us which He has not?

However, if we simply do not value the knowledge of God as utmost, we cannot get enough programs and new ideas to bridge our disconnect. We can change the lighting in our churches, bring in the cultural sensitivity course, and host all of the conferences on communicating for change. We can do all of the things and it is never enough, because we are simply at odds with the one thing that truly matters. A passage in scripture speaks to this.

"As Jesus and His disciples were on their way, He came to a village where a woman named Martha opened her home to Him. She had a sister named Mary, who sat at the Lord's feet listening to what He said. But Martha was distracted by all the preparations that had to be made. She came to Him and asked, 'Lord, don't you care that my sister has left me to do the work by myself? Tell her to help me!'

'Martha, Martha' the Lord answered, 'you are worried and upset about many things, but few things are needed — or indeed only one. Mary has chosen what is better, and it will not be taken away from her.'"

This speaks to us. One thing is needed which cannot be stripped of us, and should we lack a value for that, there are not enough programs, social justice activism, and girl pants fit for male hips to make our lives relevant. There is nothing more irrelevant than a Christian who lacks the knowledge of Christ.

A massive pit the church struggles with falling into is a quest for relevance. It is a constant pursuit for some churches to keep with the times, so to speak. It is fine if a church feels its building or music is outdated. Change it. If as a church, however, we are struggling to keep up with culture, we are already off base. There is nothing more relevant than the life of Christ on our insides bleeding into the world around us. The last thing we need to do is cover that life up in trying to be something we are not.

Christ provides solutions to our human indifferences. Jesus is the King of reconciliation. Yet, for some reason, when the issues get heated, we want to turn to Ibram X Kendi and Robin Di Angelo for answers to our cultural complexities. While Christ has the capacity to bring us all together, these people present messages which separate us.

I believe it is fine to read these people's books and seek to understand what they are saying, but it is an entirely different thing for the people of God to come under what they are saying. This is to bring the Spirit of Christ under the judgement of the world.

Think about this: we who identify with Christ value our in-Christ identity as an entirely new creature. As a new creature, I am the innocence of God and recreated after the image of Christ. Take that new creature which values that identity supremely and inform that person that he or she is either oppressor or oppressed contingent upon the color of his or her skin. What does this do? This creates confusion and ushers enmity into the unity of the Spirit.

Why subject ourselves to such nonsense? We have reality. We have answers. We've got the power!

## Christian Atonement

Christian atonement equals at-one-ment. We have seen how God has done this in Christ, bringing at-one-ment between God and man, as well as man and man. Christ is God's mediator, His peace-maker. In Christ we discover our face-to-face with God as well as our face-to-face with each other.

Because God is Father, atonement for God looks like adoption. At-one-ment for God is redemptive and it looks like the rescue of His children from a foreign captor. It looks like Jesus Christ crucified once for all.

Critical Race Theory poses a different form of atonement which is no atonement at all. Remember, Christian atonement actually equals at-one-ment. Critical Race Theory separates us according to our skin color. The only way for things to be made right is for a balancing of power. The institutional power and resource needs to be balanced, shifted from the hands of white people and distributed evenly among the people of color — except even then we will not be at peace.

Because the focus of Critical Race Theory is power and resource and not relationship, at no point does the struggle for power stop. Once the levers of power change, according to the theory, the struggle simply continues on, except power has shifted. This theory is very much militant.

We, the people of God, examine the Lamb of God and find His blood shed to be more than enough for the atonement of the human race.

## Simple Summary

In summary, I will say very simply, Critical Race Theory has no place in connection to the gospel of Jesus Christ. It is a different message in nature entirely. It would fall under the category of "hollow and deceptive philosophy". We should not go after it.

To put it plainly: the message is weak. Why would we adopt something so powerless when we have the Power of God?

The Man, Christ Jesus stands in a category of His own.

# | 5 |

# Confessing Church

"This is so that God's multi-faceted wisdom may now be
made known through the church to the rulers and authorities in the heavens,"
(Ephesians 3:10)

## Today

We are living in the greatest time in the history of existence. This is the day that the Lord has made. It is so fitting to celebrate!

There may be a "struggle" ahead for the people of God in the United States, as the truth comes out in the wash and we sift through the refuse and discard that which is inappropriate for the house of God. The "struggle", so to speak, is beautiful! It is the process of the Spirit arousing our consciousness to see what is of material, and that which is not. As the climate of the eco-system surrounding the Church heats up, that hay, wood, and stubble will inevitably be burned up.

Jesus Christ is the faithful husband of the bride. He washes us with the water of His Word and presents us immaculate in the day of revelation. Now is the time of the revelation of Jesus Christ.

There is an interaction taking place between Heaven and Earth in this moment. The Lord is filling the earth with an awareness of his Glory. The Glory Bus is cruising down the Happy Highway, and we are free at any time to get on with it.

In areas where the Church has yoked herself to worldly systems, there will be pain as people's eyes are opened and they part ways with deception, but such a glorious liberty is at hand for us in Christ! What an incredible time to be alive, and how amazing it is to be awake in this day called Today!

## Confessing Church

One aspect of the Father's awesome destiny for the people of God is revealed in Ephesians 3. The apostle expresses, "Now the multifaceted wisdom of God is being put on display through the Church, to the rulers and authorities in the heavens." (Eph 3:10) These rulers and authorities in the heavens are not angels or demons in heavenly realms. These are governing leaders in high places of authority. Jesus Christ is displaying His very wisdom to those political authorities in high places, and He is doing this in His robust expression in the Church. Oppressive times create such a stage for us.

Through powerless inventions, men seek to create what we possess in Christ. We have the goods. While messages of retributive justice cultivate an awareness of indifference, in hopes to create a just new world, we manifest effortlessly the Justice of God and shine forth hope for all. What is the justice of God? Jesus Christ is the Justice of God.

Woke-warriors obsessing over the pigment of a person's skin will seek to shape the future of our shared world according to their own ideological possessions. In magnifying race as supremely central to who a person is, they will actually create societies where we as people, red, yellow, black and white share less in common with one another.

All the while, the People of God - the Saints of the most high will stand. Amidst our day-to-day we will live in a reality wherein we acknowledge Christ as supreme and being so, we show forth His unity and our shared oneness. Jesus' disciples red, yellow, black and white will carry the culture of heaven on their shoulders and Jesus' name will be seen on their foreheads. Our laughter and shared life together will rattle the paradigms of those drowning in messages of endless indifference. The Church will emerge, leaning upon Jesus - free from the manipulations of manmade messages - manifesting heaven on earth.

The multifaceted wisdom of God is now being put on display in the people of God and those in high places are being turned on their heads to witness real, unbridled liberty.

Earlier in this work, we looked at the Nazi Coordination and the tragic error of the German Evangelical Church. We witnessed the struggle which emerged and the inevitable rise of the Confessing Church. The Confessing Church was a collective of people committed to the confessing of Jesus Christ. Joining together in a common faith, they held Jesus Christ as supreme and in doing so, they firmly resisted the cultural pressures to conform the Faith after the ways of this world.

The present move which is upon us is the move of the Confessing Church.

**YOU ARE A PART OF IT.**

Verbum Dei manet in aeternum.
**The Word of God will last for ever.?**

**Amen**

**Author**

Chris Lee is a full-time husband and father. In his occupation, he trains professional and amateur MMA competitors at his family's MMA training facility. He is an author and speak. Chris is the founder of Liberty Coalition Publications and co-founder of Inland Empire Liberty Coalition.

9 7 9 8 7 0 4 7 9 9 9 6 2